RECIPES
from the
VINEYARDS
of
NORTHERN
CALIFORNIA

Desserts

Leslie Mansfield

CELESTIALARTS
Berkeley, California

*When preparing recipes that call for egg yolks or whites, whether or not they are to be cooked, use only the highest quality, salmonella-free eggs.

CELESTIALARTS

P.O. Box 7123
Berkeley, California 94707

Distributed in Canada by Ten Speed Canada, in the United Kingdom and Europe by Airlift Books, in New Zealand by Southern Publishers Group, in Australia by Simon & Schuster Australia, in South Africa by Real Books, and in Singapore, Malaysia, Hong Kong, and Thailand by Berkeley Books.

Cover and interior design by Brad Greene
Cover photograph by Larry Kunkel
Photo styling by Veronica Randall
Public Domain Art thanks to Dover Publications

Library of Congress Card Catalog Number 99-70633

First printing, 1999
Printed in the United States

1 2 3 4 5 6 7 — 03 02 01 00 99

To Richard,
my favorite winemaker.

ACKNOWLEDGMENTS

Deepest gratitude goes to my husband Richard, who has helped me with every step—his name belongs on the title page along with mine. To my wonderful parents, Stewart and Marcia Whipple, for their unflagging confidence. To my editor Veronica Randall, who is everything I could ever want in a friend. To my editor Heather Garnos, who helps keep it all together. To Brad Greene, for another spectacular design. To Larry Kunkel, for his glorious photography.

Finally, this book would not have been possible without the cooperation of the many people at the wineries who graciously contributed their favorite recipes. I wish to thank them all for their generosity.

Table of Contents

Introduction

Just mention California wine country and thoughts of warm sunshine, vines heavy with ripening grapes, and a relaxed lifestyle come to mind. The small villages throughout the wine country each have their own personalities, as do the wineries. From rural family-run boutique wineries to large, stately wineries surrounded by a sea of vineyards, they all have one thing in common—a love for good food and wine.

This love of food and wine has resulted in an explosion of cutting-edge ideas that have defined California cuisine, incorporating the finest of Europe and Asia while drawing on the incredible local and seasonal bounty.

Entertaining is a way of life in wine country. Whether it is a formal dinner with many courses to showcase a variety of wines, or just drawing off a pitcher of new wine from the barrel to go with an impromptu picnic with neighbors, the desire to share the best they have to offer has helped shape the cuisine of California.

In the following pages you will find recipes offered from the finest wineries of northern California. Each is a reflection of their personality, whether formal or casual, and all are delicious. Each one is a taste of wine country.

ALDERBROOK VINEYARDS AND WINERY

The Dry Creek Valley, just to the west of Healdsburg, is home to Alderbrook Vineyards and Winery. Purchased by George Gillemot in 1991, Alderbrook has been on an upward course ever since. Chardonnay, Sauvignon Blanc, Gewürztraminer, Zinfandel, Pinot Noir, Syrah, Merlot, Cabernet Sauvignon, and Viognier are among the wines produced by this medal-winning winery. The quality of Alderbrook's wines can be directly traced to their stated goal: "To produce the very finest wines of the Dry Creek Valley."

MANGO &
RASPBERRY
LAYERED PUDDING

This light and fresh-tasting dessert would be fantastic after a summer barbecue.

MANGO CUSTARD:

1 cup freshly squeezed orange juice

2 packages unflavored gelatin

4 cups chopped ripe mango

1/2 cup sugar

1 cup evaporated milk

1 cup heavy cream

1 premade pound cake

1/2 cup Amaretto liqueur

2 cups raspberries

Pour the orange juice into a small saucepan. Sprinkle the gelatin over it and let soften for 5 minutes. Place over low heat and whisk until gelatin is completely dissolved. Remove from heat and set aside.

(recipe continued on next page)

In the bowl of a food processor, combine mango and sugar and process until smooth. Pour into a large bowl and stir in the evaporated milk. Stir in the orange juice mixture until smooth. Whip the cream until soft peaks form. Gently but thoroughly fold whipped cream into the mango mixture.

Slice the pound cake lengthwise into $1/2$-inch slices. Line the bottom of a trifle dish, cutting pieces of cake to fit. Sprinkle with half of the Amaretto. Spread half of the mango custard on top and sprinkle with half of the raspberries. Top with another layer of cake and sprinkle remaining Amaretto over the top. Spread remaining mango custard over the cake and sprinkle remaining raspberries on top. Cover and chill at least 4 hours before serving.

Serves 8
Serve with Alderbrook Winery
Late Harvest Sauvignon Blanc

GINGER & ALMOND STUFFED PEACHES

*It's hard to believe that such a
great-tasting dessert could be so good
for you! It's low in fat and seductively
full of flavor.*

3/4 cup slivered almonds, lightly toasted

1/3 cup packed brown sugar

1 egg white

1 teaspoon minced fresh ginger

1/2 teaspoon almond extract

1/2 teaspoon vanilla extract

3 peaches, halved and pitted

1/2 cup Alderbrook Winery Late Harvest
    Sauvignon Blanc

Preheat oven to 350° F. Lightly oil an 8 x 8-inch
baking dish.

Place almonds, brown sugar, egg white, ginger,
almond extract, and vanilla in the bowl of a food
processor. Process until coarsely chopped. With a
spoon, fill the peaches with almond mixture. Place
peaches, filling-side-up, in prepared baking dish.

(recipe continued on next page)

Pour wine into the baking dish, and baste peaches every 10 minutes while baking. Bake for about 30 to 40 minutes, or until peaches are very tender and filling is golden brown. Serve warm or cold.

Serves 6
Serve with Alderbrook Winery
Late Harvest Sauvignon Blanc

I drank at every vine.
The last was like the first.
I came upon no wine
As wonderful as thirst.

Millay

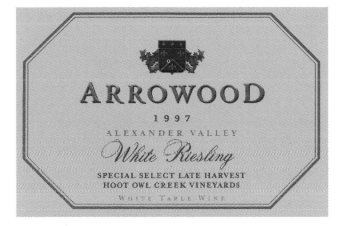

ARROWOOD
1997
ALEXANDER VALLEY
White Riesling
SPECIAL SELECT LATE HARVEST
HOOT OWL CREEK VINEYARDS
WHITE TABLE WINE

ARROWOOD VINEYARDS AND WINERY

Richard Arrowood, one of California's most renowned winemakers, and his wife and partner Alis Demers Arrowood, have crafted a winery that sits in perfect harmony with its environs. Fashioned after a New England farmhouse, the winery has often been described as a "winemaker's dream." Home to a number of wonderful, rare, and outstanding wines, Arrowood uses an intimate knowledge of the Sonoma Valley's many microclimates and terroirs to create great and complex wines.

APPLE UPSIDE-DOWN CAKE

This is a great treat to bake in the fall, when apples ripen and leaves change color in the wine country.

TOPPING:

2 tablespoons butter, melted

1/2 cup packed brown sugar

1/2 cup chopped pecans

3 apples, peeled, cored, and sliced

2 tablespoons freshly squeezed lemon juice

CAKE:

1/2 cup butter, softened

2/3 cup packed brown sugar

1/3 cup sugar

1 egg

1/2 teaspoon vanilla extract

2 cups all-purpose flour

1 teaspoon baking soda

1/2 teaspoon baking powder

1/2 teaspoon cinnamon

1/2 teaspoon nutmeg

1/2 teaspoon salt

1/2 cup buttermilk

Preheat oven to 350° F. Lightly oil a 10-inch pie plate.

For the topping: Pour the melted butter into the pie plate. Sprinkle brown sugar and pecans evenly into pie plate. Arrange apples evenly in pie plate. Sprinkle lemon juice over apples. Set aside.

For the cake: In a bowl, cream butter, brown sugar, and sugar together until light and fluffy. Beat in egg and vanilla. In a bowl, sift together flour, baking soda, baking powder, cinnamon, nutmeg, and salt. Add flour mixture alternately with buttermilk to creamed mixture. Spread batter over apples. Bake for about 45 to 50 minutes, or until a toothpick inserted in the center comes out clean. Cool in the pan for 10 minutes, then invert onto a serving plate. Serve with whipped cream.

Serves 8
Serve with Arrowood Vineyards and Winery
Special Select Late Harvest White Riesling

PEACH STREUSEL PIE

*Serve this old-fashioned treat and bring
back memories of a simpler and slower life.*

1 (10-inch) unbaked pie shell

2 pounds peaches, peeled and thickly sliced

3/4 cup sugar

1/4 teaspoon nutmeg

1 egg

2 tablespoons half-and-half

1 teaspoon vanilla extract

1/2 cup packed brown sugar

1/2 cup all-purpose flour

1/2 cup cold butter, cut into pieces

Preheat oven to 400° F.

Arrange sliced peaches in pie shell. Sprinkle sugar and nutmeg over peaches. In a small bowl, whisk together egg, half-and-half, and vanilla. Pour evenly over peaches. In a bowl, stir together brown sugar and flour. Cut in the butter until mixture resembles coarse meal. Spread mixture evenly over the peaches. Bake for 40 to 45 minutes, or until top is golden brown.

Serves 8
Serve with Arrowood Vineyards and Winery
Select Late Harvest Viognier

BELVEDERE VINEYARDS
AND WINERY

In Italian, Belvedere means "beautiful view," which aptly describes the vista from this rustic redwood winery in the Russian River Valley. The winery was built in 1982, the same year owners Bill and Sally Hambrecht bought their first piece of vineyard land high atop Bradford Mountain in Dry Creek Valley. Over the years they purchased and planted additional estate vineyards in the Dry Creek, Alexander, and Russian River Valleys in northern Sonoma County. As Bill Hambrecht often says, "Our most valuable asset is our vineyards. Good vineyards are as valuable as gold to a winery, and Belvedere has access to some of Sonoma County's best."

CREMA CATALANA

*This delicately flavored dessert from
Antonio Buenvia at Vinga Restaurant in
San Francisco is the perfect finish to a
grand meal.*

4 cups milk, divided

1/3 cup cornstarch

8 egg yolks

2/3 cup sugar

1 (4-inch) cinnamon stick

Zest of 1 lemon

6 tablespoons sugar

In a bowl, whisk together 1 cup of the milk and the cornstarch until smooth. Whisk in the egg yolks until smooth. Set aside.

In a saucepan, combine the remaining 3 cups of milk, 2/3 cup of sugar, cinnamon stick, and lemon zest. Simmer over medium heat until sugar has dissolved. Pour about one quarter of the hot milk into the egg yolk mixture and whisk until blended. Pour egg yolk mixture back into the saucepan and whisk until smooth. Simmer, stirring constantly, until thick. Take care not to let mixture boil or custard will curdle. Strain custard through a sieve into a bowl, pressing custard through with a rubber spatula.

Preheat broiler. Divide mixture into six ramekins. Sprinkle 1 tablespoon sugar evenly on top of each of the custards. Place under the broiler until the sugar caramelizes, taking care not to let them burn. Serve immediately.

Serves 6
Serve with Belvedere Vineyards and Winery
Chardonnay

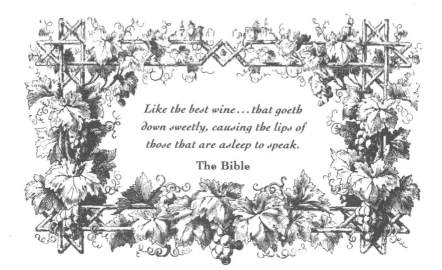

Like the best wine... that goeth down sweetly, causing the lips of those that are asleep to speak.
The Bible

CAKEBREAD CELLARS

A true family winery, Cakebread Cellars in Rutherford is one of the most creative and successful wineries in California's famed Napa Valley. Since its founding in 1973, the winery has developed a reputation for producing world-class wines and pairing them with outstanding cuisine. Dolores Cakebread, the winery's culinary director, had the vision to plant vegetable gardens at the same time their vineyards were being planted. She has been a forerunner in the development of California cuisine, which emphasizes fresh, natural, and locally grown produce to complement the wines of Cakebread Cellars.

CABERNET TRUFFLES

For the finest results, use the best quality chocolate you can find, such as Valrhona or the wine country's own Scharffen Berger.

8 ounces bittersweet chocolate, finely chopped
1/3 cup butter, softened
2 tablespoons heavy cream
1/4 cup Cakebread Cellars Cabernet Sauvignon
Unsweetened cocoa powder

🍃 In the top of a double boiler, melt the chocolate over barely simmering water. Remove from heat and whisk in the butter until smooth. Whisk in the cream. Whisk in the wine until well blended. Transfer truffle mixture to a bowl, cover, and chill until firm.

Place cocoa powder in a shallow dish. Using a melon baller, form truffle mixture into balls about 1 inch in diameter. Roll in cocoa powder to coat. Place on a plate, cover, and store in the refrigerator. Let truffles stand at room temperature for about 10 minutes before serving.

Makes about 20 truffles
Serve with Cakebread Cellars
Benchland Select Cabernet Sauvignon

CEDAR MOUNTAIN
WINERY

The creative interests of Linda and Earl Ault came to fruition in 1990, when they established Cedar Mountain Winery and began production of their award-winning wines. True to their belief that quality wines begin with the finest grapes in the vineyard, the Aults specialize in wines from fruit grown locally in the Livermore Valley. In addition to the classic Chardonnays and Bordelais varieties from these vineyards, a small amount of port—grown in the Sierra foothills— is also produced.

CRÈME
À LA CRÈME

This rich bavarois, from Sigrid Laing, is perfect to make for summer entertaining. It is made the day before, is easy to make, and is very impressive.

³/4 cup sugar

1 package unflavored gelatin

2 cups heavy cream

2 cups sour cream

1 teaspoon vanilla extract

¹/4 cup Cedar Mountain Winery
    Cabernet Royale Port

1 cup blackberries

1 cup blueberries

1 cup raspberries

🍇 Lightly oil a 6-cup ring mold.

In a heavy saucepan, whisk together the sugar and gelatin. Whisk in the cream until smooth. Let stand for 5 minutes to allow the gelatin to soften. Bring to a simmer over low heat, whisking constantly, until gelatin dissolves completely. Pour into a large bowl and let cool. Whisk in sour cream and vanilla until smooth. Pour into prepared mold, cover, and chill overnight.

(recipe continued on next page)

To serve, dip bottom of mold into hot water for a moment. Invert onto a serving plate and carefully remove mold. Drizzle with port and fill the center with berries.

Serves 6 to 8
Serve with Cedar Mountain Winery
Cabernet Royale Port

The conscious water saw its God, and blushed.

Richard Crashaw

CLOS PEGASE

1 9 9 6
PALISADES RESERVE PORT
NAPA VALLEY

ALC. 19.0% BY VOL.

CLOS PEGASE
WINERY

Driven by a desire to combine ancient traditions with modern technology, Jan Shrem founded Clos Pegase in 1983. His dream of creating a "temple to wine" has resulted in one of the most stunning and dramatic wineries in the Napa Valley. Surrounded by art, and described as "America's first monument to wine as art," Clos Pegase makes stylistic and elegant wines. Their grace does justice to the winery's namesake, Pegasus, the winged horse of Greek mythology whose hooves unleashed the sacred spring of the muses, which irrigated vines and inspired poets.

FRESH FIGS
with Lemon & Spices

*Figs have found ideal growing conditions
in the northern California wine country,
and their combination with flavorful port
is a match made in heaven.*

1 pound fresh figs

¹/3 cup Clos Pegase Winery Palisades Port

¹/3 cup water

2 lemon verbena leaves

¹/4 teaspoon anise seeds

2 whole cloves

Lightly toasted walnuts

Preheat oven to 350° F. Lightly oil an 8 x 8-inch
baking dish. Cut the stems off the figs and lightly
prick all over with a fork. Place in prepared
baking dish.

In a small saucepan, combine port and water.
Tie lemon verbena, anise seeds, and cloves in a
cheesecloth and add to saucepan. Bring to a boil,
then reduce heat to medium and simmer for 5 minutes. Pour the hot liquid over figs and place baking
dish in the oven. Bake for about 15 minutes.

Remove from oven and let figs cool in the liquid. Discard cheesecloth and spices. Serve at room temperature with the walnuts.

Serves 4 to 6
Serve with Clos Pegase Winery
Palisades Port

Of beverages, wine is the most useful,
Of curatives, the tastiest, and
Of foods, the most pleasant.

Plutarch

DE LOACH VINEYARDS

The morning fog along the Russian River Valley, a product of marine influence, is instrumental for the quality of Cecil and Christine De Loach's estate-grown wines. This cooling influence in the heat of late summer allows their vines to fully develop their fruit while maintaining acidity and elegance. Cecil and Christine De Loach's personal connection to their vineyards and cellar ensures a consistency of style and excellence in quality year after year.

COUNTRY PEACH TART *with* *Gewürztraminer Glaze*

The floral aromas of Gewürztraminer ideally complement the luscious flavor of tree-ripened peaches.

CRUST:

1 1/3 cups all-purpose flour

1 teaspoon salt

1 teaspoon sugar

1/4 cup cold butter, cut into pieces

1/4 cup shortening

1/4 cup cold water

FILLING:

2/3 cup sugar

3 tablespoons cornstarch

1/3 cup De Loach Late Harvest Gewürztraminer

3 pounds peaches, peeled and thickly sliced
(about 6 cups)

1 tablespoon sugar

(recipe continued on next page)

For the crust: In the bowl of a food processor, combine flour, salt, and sugar and pulse to blend. Add butter and shortening and pulse until mixture resembles coarse meal. Drizzle the water evenly over the mixture and pulse a few times, just until dough forms a ball. Gather dough into a ball and flatten into a disc. Wrap in plastic wrap and chill at least one hour.

For the filling: In a large bowl, whisk together the sugar and cornstarch. Whisk in the wine until smooth. Stir in the peaches and let stand 20 minutes.

Preheat oven to 450° F. Turn dough out onto a lightly floured board and roll out to fit a 10-inch pie plate. Prick dough all over with a fork and fit gently into pie plate. Stir peaches and pour into pie shell. Crimp the edges decoratively. Line oven rack with foil to catch any drips. Bake for 20 minutes. Lower temperature to 375 ° F and bake an additional 30 to 35 minutes, or until crust is golden brown and peaches are bubbly. Serve warm.

Serves 8
Serve with De Loach Vineyards
Late Harvest Gewürztraminer

DOMAINE CHARBAY WINERY AND DISTILLERY

Domaine Charbay, a truly artisanal distillery and winery, is the home of master distiller and winemaker Miles Karakasevic. With his wife Susan and their two adult children, Marko and Lara, he produces astounding small production releases of wines, ports, eaux de vie, liqueurs, and exquisite brandies from their traditional alembic still and winery. Located high above St. Helena atop Spring Mountain, the "still on the hill" is often the site of spontaneous gatherings of family and friends. The enjoyment of simple food along with their hand made wine and spirits is part of the convivial hospitality, which has become their trademark.

BREAD PUDDING
with Charbay Sauce

Charbay is a blend of toasty Chardonnay and brandy liqueur from the like-named Domaine Charbay.

1 1/2 cups sugar

3 eggs

1 tablespoon vanilla extract

1 teaspoon cinnamon

1 1/4 cups milk

1 loaf day-old French bread, cut into 1/2-inch cubes

1 cup dried cranberries

1/2 cup chopped dried apricots

CHARBAY SAUCE:

1/2 cup butter

3/4 cup powdered sugar

1 egg

3/4 cup Charbay

🍇 Lightly oil a 13 x 9-inch baking dish. In a large bowl, beat the sugar and eggs together until light. Beat in the vanilla and cinnamon. Stir in the milk until smooth. Stir in the bread cubes, cranberries, and apricots until evenly moistened. Pour into prepared baking dish and let stand for 1 hour.

For the sauce: In a small saucepan, melt butter over medium-low heat. Add powdered sugar and whisk until sugar is completely dissolved. Remove from heat and whisk in the egg until smooth. Whisk in the Charbay. Set aside.

Preheat oven to 350° F. Bake the pudding for about 1 hour to 1 hour and 15 minutes, or until golden brown and set in the middle. Serve warm with Charbay sauce.

Serves 8 to 10
Serve with a snifter of Charbay

27

1994 DRY CHENIN BLANC
California
Alcohol 13.0% by volume

DRY CREEK VINEYARD

Dry Creek Vineyard was the first new winery to be established in the Dry Creek Valley of Sonoma after Prohibition. Synonymous with fine winemaking, Dry Creek Vineyard draws upon over thirty-five different vineyards to produce their wines, matching the particular soils and microclimates of each site to the varieties that do best.

CHERRY CHENIN SOUP

*This delightful chilled soup would be
perfect at an alfresco lunch.*

4 cups pitted fresh cherries, divided

2 cups Dry Creek Vineyards Chenin Blanc

2 cups water

1/2 cup sugar

2 tablespoons freshly squeezed orange juice

1 teaspoon finely minced orange zest

1 teaspoon freshly squeezed lemon juice

1/2 teaspoon almond extract

1 tablespoon plus 1 teaspoon cornstarch

3 tablespoons cold water

Sour cream

In a large saucepan, combine 2 cups of the
cherries, wine, 2 cups water, sugar, orange juice,
orange zest, lemon juice, and almond extract. Bring
to a boil, then reduce heat to low, cover, and simmer for about 15 minutes, or until cherries are very
tender. Purée mixture and return to pan.

(recipe continued on next page)

In a small bowl, stir together cornstarch with 3 tablespoons cold water. Bring soup to a simmer over medium heat. Whisk in cornstarch mixture and, stirring constantly, simmer until thickened. Stir in reserved cherries and bring back to a simmer. Remove from heat and cool to room temperature, then cover and refrigerate until very cold. Serve with a dollop of sour cream.

Serves 6
Serve with Dry Creek Vineyards
Chenin Blanc

I rather like bad wine...
one gets so bored with good wine.
Disraeli

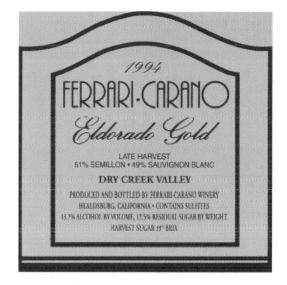

1994

FERRARI·CARANO

Eldorado Gold

LATE HARVEST
51% SEMILLON • 49% SAUVIGNON BLANC

DRY CREEK VALLEY

PRODUCED AND BOTTLED BY FERRARI-CARANO WINERY
HEALDSBURG, CALIFORNIA • CONTAINS SULFITES
13.7% ALCOHOL BY VOLUME, 12.5% RESIDUAL SUGAR BY WEIGHT
HARVEST SUGAR 39° BRIX

FERRARI-CARANO
VINEYARDS AND WINERY

Villa Fiore, or "House of Flowers," at Ferrari-Carano is one of the most spectacular wineries and visitors' centers in the northern California wine country. Designed to reflect the proud Italian heritage of the Carano family, Villa Fiore houses state-of-the art kitchens, which are used to educate professionals as well as consumers in the enjoyment of Ferrari-Carano wines. Ferrari-Carano draws its grapes from fourteen winery-owned vineyards over a fifty-mile area, from Alexander Valley in the north to the Carneros district in the south. This exceptional supply of fruit allows the winemaker to produce the highly stylized wines for which Ferrari-Carano is known.

RASPBERRY & ZINFANDEL POACHED PEARS

A whole kaleidoscope of flavors greets you in this rich and scrumptious dessert.

1 1/4 cups mascarpone cheese

3 tablespoons powdered sugar

2 tablespoons Ferrari-Carano Winery
    Eldorado Gold

5 ripe but firm Bartlett pears

2 cups raspberries

3 cups Ferrari-Carano Winery Zinfandel

1 cup water

2 strips lemon zest

2 strips orange zest

5 whole peppercorns

1 (3-inch) cinnamon stick

1/2 vanilla bean

1 sprig fresh basil

1 cup whole raspberries and 10 mint sprigs,
    for garnish

In a small bowl, whisk together mascarpone, powdered sugar, and Eldorado Gold wine until smooth. Set aside.

Peel the pears. Cut in half lengthwise and scoop out the cores with a melon baller.

In the bowl of a food processor, purée 2 cups of the raspberries. Strain through a fine sieve and discard the seeds. In a large saucepan, combine the raspberry purée, Zinfandel, water, lemon zest, orange zest, peppercorns, cinnamon stick, vanilla bean, and basil and bring to a boil. Reduce heat to medium-low and add the pears. Poach the pears until tender. With a slotted spoon, remove pears and set aside. Increase heat to medium and simmer until poaching liquid is reduced to 2 cups. Strain through a fine sieve and ladle syrup into shallow serving bowls. Fill the centers of the pears with the mascarpone mixture. Place pears in the bowls and garnish with whole raspberries and mint.

Serves 8 to 10
Serve with Ferrari-Carano Winery
Eldorado Gold

FETZER VINEYARDS

"Live right, Eat right, Pick the right grapes"™ sig-
nifies the Fetzer Vineyards philosophy toward wine
production and living in general. Fetzer has dedi-
cated itself to being an environmentally and socially
conscious grower, producer, and marketer of wines
of the highest quality, and, to that end, farms 360
acres of certified organic grapes. Their award-win-
ning wines run the gamut from Johannisberg Ries-
ling to reserve Cabernet Sauvignon. Based in Men-
docino County, Fetzer is one of the north coast's
finest producers of premium wine.

CHOCOLATE TRUFFLE TORTE

This "death by chocolate" cake is from John Ash, well-known author and executive chef at Fetzer Vineyards.

TORTE:

1¼ cups butter

10 ounces semisweet chocolate, chopped

9 egg yolks

1⅓ cups sugar, divided

5 egg whites

⅛ teaspoon salt

CHOCOLATE GLAZE:

¾ cup heavy cream

6 ounces semisweet chocolate, chopped

❧ Preheat oven to 350° F. Butter a 10-inch springform pan and line the bottom with parchment paper.

For the torte: In the top of a double boiler, melt butter and chocolate together over barely simmering water. Whisk until smooth and let cool.

(recipe continued on next page)

In a large bowl, beat the egg yolks and $2/3$ cup of the sugar until pale in color and thick. Fold the chocolate mixture into the yolk mixture.

In a large bowl, beat the egg whites and salt together until soft peaks form. Gradually add the remaining $2/3$ cup of sugar, beating constantly until all is incorporated. Gently fold egg whites into the chocolate mixture thoroughly but taking care not to deflate the mixture. Pour batter into prepared springform pan. Bake for about 1 hour, or until set in the middle. Remove from oven and cool in the pan, then cover and chill thoroughly.

For the glaze: In a small saucepan, heat the cream over medium-low until it almost simmers. Remove from heat and add the chocolate. Whisk until smooth.

Remove the springform pan and invert the torte onto a 10-inch round of cardboard. Place a rack on a baking sheet and place the torte on the rack. Peel off parchment and brush off any crumbs. With a small spatula, spread the glaze over the top and sides of the torte. Pour the remaining glaze over the top. Chill to set the glaze. Serve in thin wedges.

Serves 12
Serve with Fetzer Vineyards
Cabernet Sauvignon

LEMON-GLAZED PERSIMMON BARS

These chewy bars come to us courtesy of pioneering chef John Ash, whose cookbook From the Earth to the Table *has helped define California wine country cuisine.*

LEMON GLAZE:

1 cup sifted powdered sugar

3 tablespoons freshly squeezed lemon juice

1 cup Hachiya persimmon pulp

1 teaspoon soda water (club soda or seltzer)

1 egg

1 cup sugar

1/2 cup vegetable oil

1 3/4 cups all-purpose flour

1 teaspoon salt

1 teaspoon cinnamon

1/2 teaspoon ground cloves

1/2 teaspoon freshly grated nutmeg

3/4 cup chopped walnuts, almonds, or other nuts

3/4 cup coarsely chopped dates

(recipe continued on next page)

🍃 Preheat oven to 350° F. Lightly oil and flour a jelly roll pan.

For the glaze: In a saucepan, combine the powdered sugar and lemon juice. Bring to a simmer over medium heat and stir until the sugar melts. Remove from heat and set aside.

In a small bowl, whisk together the persimmon pulp and the soda water and set aside. In a bowl, beat the egg lightly. Add the sugar and oil and mix well. Stir in the persimmon mixture until smooth. In a bowl, stir together the flour, salt, cinnamon, cloves, and nutmeg. Add flour mixture to the persimmon mixture and stir until smooth. Stir in walnuts and dates. Spread batter into the prepared jelly roll pan. Bake for about 25 minutes, or until golden brown. Glaze while hot with the lemon glaze. Cut into bars.

Makes 36 bars
Serve with Fetzer Vineyards
Johannisberg Riesling

GLORIA FERRER
CHAMPAGNE CAVES

Founded by José Ferrer, son of Pedro Ferrer Bosch, the Spanish-Catalan founder of Freixenet, Gloria Ferrer Champagne Caves was opened to the public in July of 1986. Named for José Ferrer's beloved wife, Gloria, the winery has been winning awards and the accolades of wine critics ever since. Located within the cool Carneros appellation, the beautiful building with stucco walls, arched windows, and overhanging balconies is a piece of the proud history of old Spain.

STRAWBERRIES
AU GRATIN

*This elegant dessert is the perfect end
to a summer meal.*

1 pound strawberries, sliced

1/2 cup heavy cream

2 egg yolks

1/4 cup sugar

1/2 cup Gloria Ferrer Champagne Caves
    Blanc de Noirs

Lightly oil a quiche dish. Arrange strawberries in
the dish. Set aside.

In a bowl, beat cream until soft peaks form.
Set aside.

In the top of a double boiler, whisk egg yolks
and sugar together. Add the wine slowly, whisking
constantly. Cook over simmering water, whisking
constantly, until mixture doubles in volume. Remove
from heat and fold in whipped cream. Spread
mixture evenly over strawberries. Preheat the broiler.
Place under the broiler to barely brown the top, take
care that it does not burn. Serve immediately.

Serves 4
*Serve with Gloria Ferrer Champagne Caves
Blanc de Noirs*

BRUTOCAO
CELLARS

The Lion of St. Mark is the symbol the Brutocao family chose for their 475-acre vineyard and winery in southern Mendocino County. It symbolizes family tradition and quality, along with artistic passion for the wines produced. No synthetic chemicals are used in the vineyard; the red wines are unfined and unfiltered, and the whites are barrel fermented and aged sur-lie (upon natural sediments) until bottled. Judicious use of new oak serves to complement—not cover up—the natural flavors of the Mendocino grapes. In keeping with their Italian heritage, the Brutocao family truly believes their wines are meant to be enjoyed with food.

CABERNET PEARS

This is an easy, elegant, and refreshing dessert that can be made in advance and is perfect after a heavy meal.

4 1/2 cups Brutocao Cellars Cabernet Sauvignon

3/4 cup sugar

1 tablespoon minced orange zest

1 teaspoon whole black peppercorns

1 bay leaf

4 ripe but firm pears, peeled, halved, and cored

2 tablespoons cornstarch

2 tablespoons orange juice

Vanilla ice cream

In a saucepan, combine wine, sugar, orange zest, peppercorns, and bay leaf. Bring to a boil and add pears. Reduce heat to low, cover, and simmer for about 10 minutes, or until tender. Remove from heat and let cool to room temperature. Chill pears in the poaching liquid overnight.

Remove pears, slice and fan onto eight shallow bowls. Set aside.

Place poaching liquid back on the stove and simmer over medium heat until mixture is reduced by half. In a small bowl, whisk together cornstarch and orange juice. Whisk into reduced wine mixture and simmer, whisking constantly, until sauce has thickened.

Place a scoop of ice cream next to pears and drizzle sauce on top. Serve immediately.

Serves 8
Serve with Brutocao Cellars Mistell

Worries enough come all the time,
And the cure therefore is the
beloved vine.

Johann Wolfgang von Goethe

HUSCH VINEYARDS

Husch Vineyards is a small family winery and the first bonded winery located in the Anderson Valley appellation of Mendocino County in northern California, a picturesque two-and-a-half hour drive north of San Francisco. All Husch wines are made from grapes grown in the family-owned vineyards. Some of the wines are distributed throughout the United States, but many are available only locally or at their tasting room. Quality is the key word at the winery. It shows in the care that goes into growing fine grapes, in the attention given in each step of the winemaking process, and in the time given to visitors who come to the winery for tastings.

MIXED NUT
TORTE

*Cap your next dinner party with this
incredibly rich pièce de résistance.*

4 ounces almonds

4 ounces hazelnuts

4 ounces pecans

4 ounces walnuts

1 1/2 cups sugar

1 cup butter, softened

5 eggs

2 tablespoons orange liqueur

2 tablespoons orange marmalade

1 teaspoon baking powder

1/2 cup vanilla wafer crumbs

Powdered sugar

(recipe continued on next page)

🍂 Preheat oven to 350° F. Lightly oil a 9-inch cake pan and line the bottom with parchment paper.

Place nuts on an ungreased baking sheet. Bake for about 5 to 7 minutes, or until lightly toasted. Remove from oven and cool. Place cooled nuts in the bowl of a food processor and process until finely ground.

In a large bowl, beat sugar and butter together until light. Add the nuts and beat until well blended. Add eggs, one at a time, beating well after each addition. Add orange liqueur, orange marmalade, baking powder, and vanilla wafer crumbs and beat until well blended. Pour batter into prepared pan. Bake for about 1 hour, or until a toothpick inserted in the center comes out clean. Cool completely in the pan. Run a knife around the edge of the torte and invert onto a serving plate. Dust with powdered sugar.

Serves 12
Serve with Husch Vineyards
Muscat Canelli

ALMOND GINGER BISCOTTI

Biscotti are great to serve between lunch and dinner when guests drop by. They are even better when paired with a glass of late harvest Gewürztraminer.

2 ¹/2 cups all-purpose flour

1 cup sugar

¹/4 cup finely minced crystallized ginger

¹/2 teaspoon baking powder

¹/2 teaspoon baking soda

¹/2 teaspoon salt

3 eggs

1 teaspoon vanilla extract

³/4 cup whole almonds

Heavy cream

Preheat oven to 350° F. Line a baking sheet with parchment paper.

In a large bowl, stir together flour, sugar, crystallized ginger, baking powder, baking soda, and salt. In a small bowl, whisk together eggs and vanilla. Add to flour mixture and stir until blended. Stir in the almonds. Turn dough out onto a lightly

(recipe continued on next page)

floured board. Dough will be very sticky. Shape dough into a log and flatten slightly. Transfer dough to prepared baking sheet. Brush with cream. Bake for about 50 minutes, or until golden brown. Remove from oven and let cool.

Reduce oven temperature to 300° F. Transfer log to a cutting board and cut 1/2-inch-thick diagonal slices. Place the biscotti, cut-side-down, on the baking sheet and bake 5 minutes. Turn biscotti over and bake an additional 5 minutes. Cool on racks.

Makes about 36 biscotti
Serve with Husch Vineyards
Late Harvest Gewürztraminer

IRON HORSE
VINEYARDS

Ten miles from the Pacific coast and sixty-five miles north of San Francisco lies Iron Horse Vineyards, named for the railroad stop it once was. Barry and Audrey Sterling, along with their partner and vineyard manager Forrest Tancer, have developed Iron Horse into one of the premier wineries in the United States. In addition to their well-known and sought-after sparkling wines, they produce outstanding still wines from their vineyards in Sonoma County's Green and Alexander Valleys. The Sterlings and Forrest all live on their land and give daily care and attention to their vineyards, thus assuring consistency and high quality wines.

CHERRY GALETTE

Mark Malicki serves this rustic, free-form galette warm with vanilla ice cream.

CRUST:

2 1/2 cups all-purpose flour

2 tablespoons sugar

1/2 teaspoon salt

1 cup cold butter, cut into pieces

1/4 cup cold water

1 egg yolk

FILLING:

4 cups pitted cherries

1/4 cup sugar

2 tablespoons butter, cut into pieces

🍇 Preheat oven to 400° F. Line a rimmed baking sheet with parchment paper.

For the crust: In a large bowl, stir together flour, sugar, and salt. Cut in the butter until mixture resembles coarse meal. In a small bowl, whisk together water and egg yolk. Stir into flour mixture until dough holds together. Gather dough into a ball and flatten into a disk. Cover with plastic wrap and chill.

For the filling: In a large bowl, stir together cherries and sugar. Set aside.

Remove dough from refrigerator and turn out onto a lightly floured board. Roll out to about 1/4-inch thick. Transfer dough to the prepared baking sheet. Leaving a 3-inch border, put cherries in the center of the dough. Dot with butter. Fold the edges of the dough over the cherries and towards the center. Bake for about 40 minutes, or until crust is golden brown and filling is hot and bubbly.

Serves 8
Serve with Iron Horse Vineyards
Blanc de Blancs

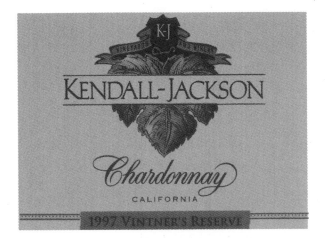

KENDALL-JACKSON
WINERY

In 1974, Jess Jackson and his family purchased an 85-acre pear ranch near Lakeport in northern California. By 1982, the ranch was a vineyard, the barn was a tasting room, and the pasture was a winery. Meanwhile, they studied the premium vineyards that span California's cool coastal growing regions and discovered the wonderful spectrum of flavors produced by the same grape varietal grown in different locations. Why not use this exciting diversity? Why not blend the best grapes from the best vineyards to produce unique wines with layers of depth and complexity? Their first Chardonnay was made in 1982, from vineyards in Santa Barbara, Monterey, Sonoma, and Lake Counties. This wine was named "Best American Chardonnay" by the American Wine Competition. Their concept of blending the best with the best was affirmed and to this day continues to be the reason their wines are noted for their consistency and complexity, vintage after vintage.

CHÈVRE CHEESECAKE
with Biscotti Crust

Tess McDonough created this unusual cheesecake that has a beguiling hint of garden herbs.

CRUST:

3/4 cup butter, softened

3/4 cup powdered sugar

1 egg

1 cup all-purpose flour

1/2 cup vanilla biscotti crumbs

1/4 cup ground walnuts

FILLING:

8 ounces cream cheese, at room temperature

4 ounces chèvre (soft goat cheese)

1/4 cup sugar

2 eggs

1/4 cup Kendall-Jackson Winery Chardonnay

1/2 teaspoon finely minced fresh rosemary

1/2 teaspoon salt

TOPPING:

2 pints raspberries

3/4 cup sugar

1/2 cup Kendall-Jackson Winery Chardonnay

(recipe continued on next page)

🍃 Preheat oven to 300° F.

For the crust: In a bowl, beat butter, powdered sugar, and egg together until smooth. Add flour, biscotti crumbs, and walnuts and stir until well blended. Press mixture into the bottom and 1 inch up the sides of a 10-inch springform pan.

For the filling: In a large bowl, beat together cream cheese and chèvre until well blended. Beat in sugar until smooth. Add eggs, one at a time, beating well after each addition. Add wine, rosemary, and salt and beat until smooth, scraping sides of the bowl often. Pour mixture into crust. Bake for about 1 hour, or until cheesecake starts to pull away from the sides and center is set. Cool to room temperature, then cover and chill overnight.

For the topping: In a saucepan, combine raspberries, sugar, and wine and bring to a boil. Reduce heat to medium-low and simmer until mixture is slightly thickened. Remove from heat and chill.

To serve, carefully remove the band from the springform pan. Carefully slide a long spatula under the crust of the cheesecake and slide onto a serving platter. Serve with raspberry topping.

Serves 12
Serve with Kendall-Jackson Winery Chardonnay

54

KENWOOD VINEYARDS

At Kenwood Vineyards, each vineyard lot is handled separately within the winery to preserve its individuality. Such "small lot" winemaking allows the winemaker to bring each lot of wine to its fullest potential. This style of winemaking is evident in the quality of Kenwood's special bottlings. From the Jack London Vineyard series, whose grapes come from the historical lava-terraced vineyards of the Jack London Ranch, to the Artist Series Cabernet Sauvignon, whose labels each year feature the work of a renowned artist, Kenwood's reds show Sonoma at its best.

MERLOT
BROWNIES

*These decadently rich brownies are
from Carlo Di Clemente. They illustrate
just how good a combination red wine
and chocolate is.*

1 cup Kenwood Vineyards Merlot

3/4 cup butter

4 ounces unsweetened chocolate

2 cups sugar

3 eggs

1 teaspoon vanilla extract

1 cup all-purpose flour

1 cup coarsely chopped pecans

Preheat oven to 350° F. Lightly butter a
13 x 9-inch baking pan.

In a small saucepan, simmer the wine over
medium heat until reduced to 1/4 cup. Pour into a
large bowl and set aside.

In the top of a double boiler, melt butter and
chocolate together over simmering water. Pour into
wine and whisk until smooth.

In the top of a double boiler, whisk together sugar, eggs, and vanilla over simmering water until very light and thick. Pour into chocolate mixture and whisk until smooth. Stir in flour and 1/2 cup of the pecans. Pour into prepared pan and sprinkle remaining 1/2 cup pecans on top. Bake for 40 to 45 minutes, or until a toothpick inserted in the center comes out clean. Cut into 2-inch squares.

Makes about 36 squares
Serve with Kenwood Vineyards
Merlot

When the wine goes in,
strange things come out.
Schiller

KUNDE ESTATE WINERY

The Kunde Estate winery may look nineteenth century on the outside, but it is definitely twenty-first century on the inside. The 17,000-square-foot facility features all the latest technology, planned for maximum flexibility and efficiency. The 350,000-gallon capacity winery features specialized crushing equipment that allows the winemaker to direct whole clusters to the press, a real advantage in white wine production, or elect whole berry fermentation for enhanced fruity character in Zinfandel or Merlot.

SHERRY TORTE

This delightful cake from Leslie Kunde tastes even better the next day.

4 eggs, separated

3/4 cup sugar, divided

1 cup all-purpose flour

1 teaspoon baking powder

1/2 teaspoon salt

1/3 cup butter, melted

1 teaspoon vanilla extract

SHERRY SAUCE:

1 cup sugar

1 cup water

1/4 cup dry sherry

1/2 cup sweetened flaked coconut, lightly toasted

(recipe continued on next page)

⟡ Preheat oven to 375° F. Lightly oil an 8 x 8-inch baking pan.

In a large bowl, beat the egg yolks with 1/2 cup of the sugar until pale in color and thick. In a separate bowl, beat the egg whites until soft peaks form. Gradually beat in remaining 1/4 cup sugar until all is incorporated. Fold into yolk mixture. Sift the flour, baking powder, and salt together and fold into egg mixture. Fold in the melted butter and vanilla. Pour batter into prepared pan. Bake for about 30 minutes, or until a toothpick inserted in the center comes out clean.

For the sauce: In a saucepan, cook sugar and water together over high heat until a candy thermometer reaches 235° F. Remove from heat and whisk in sherry.

When torte comes out of the oven, poke holes all over with a skewer. Pour the sherry sauce evenly over the cake. Sprinkle with toasted coconut.

Serves 6
Serve with Kunde Estate Winery
Chardonnay

MARK WEST ESTATE
VINEYARD AND WINERY

Certified organic since 1990, Mark West Estate Vineyard and Winery is located where the cooling effects of the nearby Pacific Ocean and the fogs of San Pablo Bay provide ideal growing conditions for their fruit. Their 66 acres of Chardonnay, Pinot Noir, Gewürztraminer, and Merlot, whose original plantings date back to 1974, show restrained elegance and delicate, yet multilayered fruit. Ideal to show off the nuances of a subtly seasoned cuisine, the wines of Mark West are proof positive that wine enhances a fine meal.

LATE HARVEST GEWÜRZTRAMINER ICE CREAM *with Caramel Sauce & Fresh Berries*

If you don't already have an ice cream maker, this recipe will surely inspire you to buy one.

ICE CREAM:

3 egg yolks

1/2 cup half-and-half

1/2 cup sugar

1 1/2 cups heavy cream

1 cup Mark West Winery Late Harvest Gewürztraminer

CARAMEL SAUCE:

1 1/2 cups sugar

1/2 cup water

1 cup heavy cream

Fresh berries in season, such as raspberries or strawberries

For the ice cream: In a small bowl, whisk the egg yolks lightly. Set aside. In a saucepan, whisk together the half-and-half and sugar over medium-low heat until sugar dissolves. Pour half of the mixture into the egg yolks and whisk until blended. Pour egg yolk mixture back into the saucepan and whisk until blended. Simmer over low heat, stirring constantly with a wooden spoon, until mixture coats the back of the spoon. Strain through a fine sieve into a bowl. Whisk in cream and wine. Chill thoroughly, then pour into an ice cream maker and freeze according to manufacturer's directions.

For the sauce: In a saucepan, bring sugar and water to a boil, swirling the pan often to blend. Cook until sugar caramelizes and turns deep golden brown. Remove from heat and pour in the cream, take care since it may splatter a bit. Whisk until smooth, then let cool.

Serve ice cream topped with caramel sauce and berries.

Makes about 1 quart
Serve with Mark West Winery
Late Harvest Gewürztraminer

MARKHAM VINEYARDS

Markham Vineyards has, for over twenty years, rewarded oenophiles with wines of a consistency and level of quality seldom matched in the Napa Valley. From its historic stone winery, built in 1873 by Jean Laurent, an immigrant from Bordeaux, Markham crafts outstanding wines that are unpretentious in style and are meant to be enjoyed. Vineyards from San Pablo Bay north to Calistoga provide a wealth of different growing conditions for both their white and red wines.

MASCARPONE MOUSSE & CRANBERRY PARFAIT

Linda Thomas Catering developed this festive and elegant holiday dessert for us.

CRANBERRY COMPOTE:

1$\frac{1}{4}$ cups sugar

$\frac{1}{2}$ cup cranberry-raspberry juice

10 ounces fresh whole cranberries

MASCARPONE MOUSSE:

8 ounces mascarpone cheese, at room
   temperature

2 egg yolks

$\frac{1}{3}$ cup powdered sugar, sifted

1 tablespoon orange liqueur

Zest of 1 orange, finely minced

1 cup heavy cream, whipped until stiff

FOR GARNISH:

1 cup heavy cream, whipped until stiff

Mint sprigs

(recipe continued on next page)

MONTICELLO
VINEYARDS

Monticello, a 20,000-case winery just north of the town of Napa, was built in the style of Thomas Jefferson's personal estate in recognition of his contribution to American wine and food. Winery founder Jay Corley's family traces its connection back to 1640 and to Bedford County, Virginia, the same county where Jefferson advocated freedom for a new America. The Jefferson House at Monticello Vineyards stands as a symbol of excellence and quality in winemaking. The Oak Knoll region north of the town of Napa is home to Monticello's Chardonnay and Pinot Noir. Corley chose that area to plant Burgundian varieties because it is cooler than the upper valley; he reserves his State Lane Vineyard further north in warmer Yountville to plant Cabernet Sauvignon

CHOCOLATE TRUFFLE CRÈME BRÛLÉE

*A very rich, smooth chocolate dessert
that pairs beautifully with
Cabernet Sauvignon.*

3 eggs

3 egg yolks

2 2/3 cups heavy cream

2/3 cup sugar

8 ounces semisweet chocolate chips

1 tablespoon vanilla extract

1/2 cup sugar, divided

Preheat oven to 350° F. In a large bowl, whisk
together eggs and egg yolks. Set aside.

In a saucepan, combine cream, 2/3 cup sugar,
chocolate chips, and vanilla. Over medium-low
heat, whisk until chocolate melts. Whisk over
medium-low heat until chocolate melts. Strain
mixture through a fine sieve and pour into eight
ramekins. Place ramekins in a baking pan and add
enough hot water to come halfway up the sides of
the ramekins. Bake for about 20 minutes, or until
custard is just set. Cool to room temperature but
do not refrigerate.

(recipe continued on next page)

Preheat broiler. Sprinkle about 1 tablespoon sugar evenly on top of each of the custards. Place under the broiler until the sugar caramelizes, taking care not to let them burn. Serve immediately.

Serves 8
Serve with Monticello Vineyards Corley Reserve

*Fill high the bowl
with Samian wine!*

Byron

ALMOND PRALINE CHEESECAKE *with* *Cinnamon Graham Crust*

Pralines and cheesecake—oh my!
This has to be one of the most incredible
cheesecakes ever invented.

ALMOND PRALINE:

$1/2$ cup sugar

$1/4$ cup water

$3/4$ cup chopped almonds

CINNAMON GRAHAM CRUST:

$2 1/4$ cups (8 ounces) graham cracker crumbs

1 teaspoon cinnamon

$1/2$ cup butter, melted

TOPPING:

2 cups sour cream

$1/4$ cup sugar

1 teaspoon vanilla extract

FILLING:

$2 1/2$ pounds cream cheese, at room temperature

$3/4$ cup sugar

2 eggs

1 teaspoon vanilla extract

(recipe continued on next page)

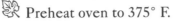 Preheat oven to 375° F.

For the praline: Lightly oil a baking sheet. In a small saucepan, bring sugar and water to a boil, swirling the pan often to blend. Cook until sugar caramelizes and turns a deep golden brown. Stir in the almonds. Pour onto prepared baking sheet. Allow to cool completely, then chop coarsely and set aside.

For the crust: Place graham cracker crumbs and cinnamon in the bowl of a food processor. Pulse a few times to mix ingredients. Add the melted butter and pulse to blend. Press the mixture into the bottom and halfway up the sides of a 10-inch springform pan. Set aside.

For the topping: In a bowl, whisk together the sour cream, sugar, and vanilla until smooth. Set aside.

For the filling: In a large bowl, beat the cream cheese and the sugar together until smooth, scraping the sides of the bowl often. Add eggs, one at a time, beating well after each addition. Beat in the vanilla. Stir in the reserved almond praline. Pour batter into the prepared crust and place springform pan on a baking sheet. Bake for about 30 minutes, then remove from oven and cool 10 minutes. Spread topping evenly over cheesecake and return to oven. Bake an additional 10 to 15 minutes, or until almost set in the center. Cool to room temperature, then cover and chill overnight.

Remove cheesecake from refrigerator. Carefully remove the band of the springform pan. Slide a long spatula under the crust of the cheesecake and slide onto a serving plate.

Serves 12
Serve with Monticello Vineyards
Chateau M

*Is not old wine wholesomest,
old pippins toothsomest, old wood burn
brightest, old linen wash whitest?
Old soldiers, sweethearts surest, and old
lovers are soundest.*
John Webster

NAVARRO VINEYARDS

There are few wineries in northern California that have had the success with their wines that Navarro Vineyards has experienced. Visitors to this winery's tasting room, when asking about one of the current vintages, are often sorrowfully informed, "Sorry, the Chardonnay and Pinot Noir have sold out." This speaks to the absolute quality standards that Ted Bennet and Deborah Cahn have set for the wines they make. Known for their incredible delicacy and fruit, Navarro's wines are not just your standard California varietals. In addition to their outstanding Pinot Noir and Chardonnay, they take great pains to keep other, lesser-known wines in production. Their Chenin Blanc, White Riesling, and Gewürztraminers are known to wine lovers as among the world's finest, and their Sauvignon Blanc, Pinot Gris, Muscat Blanc, and Valdiguié never fail to charm first-time tasters.

CANDIED GINGER & ALMOND PEARS

*Pears are one of the late summer treats
that herald the beginning of autumn.*

3 cups water

1 tablespoon freshly squeezed lemon juice

3 ripe large pears

1/2 cup heavy cream

1/4 cup chopped almonds, lightly toasted

2 teaspoons minced candied ginger

In a bowl, combine water and lemon juice.
Peel pears and cut in half lengthwise. Scoop out
the cores with a melon baller. Place pears in the
water to prevent them from browning. In a bowl,
beat cream until stiff. Fold in almonds and ginger.
Drain pears and gently dry them with paper
towels. Fill the centers with the whipped cream
mixture.

Serves 6
Serve with Navarro Vineyards
Cluster Select Late Harvest Gewürztraminer

RMS ALAMBIC
DISTILLERY

Located among the rolling hillsides of the Carneros region of the Napa Valley, RMS Distillery practices traditional methods of brandy distillation. Six different varieties of grapes are double distilled in classic alambic pot stills imported from Cognac. The classic Cognac method of distilling on the lees captures the essence of the ripe California fruit and maximizes the complexity of their fine brandies. Extended aging in French Limousin Oak barrels imparts toasty spice and rich vanilla flavors.

PLUM PUDDING

You can prepare this holiday tradition up to three weeks in advance. Simply unmold, wrap in plastic, and store in your refrigerator.

1 cup currants

3/4 cup golden raisins

1/3 cup RMS Alambic Distillery Special Reserve Brandy

3/4 cup packed brown sugar

1/2 cup ground almonds

1/4 cup fine dry breadcrumbs

2 tablespoons all-purpose flour

1/2 teaspoon baking powder

1/2 teaspoon cinnamon

1/2 teaspoon salt

1/4 teaspoon mace

2 ounces suet (preferably from veal kidney fat), finely chopped

1/3 cup milk, scalded

2 egg yolks, lightly beaten

2 egg whites, beaten until stiff

3 tablespoons RMS Alambic Distillery Special Reserve Brandy

(recipe continued on next page)

In a bowl, combine currants, raisins, and 1/3 cup brandy and let sit overnight.

Butter and flour a 1-quart pudding mold with a tight-fitting lid.

In a large bowl, stir together brown sugar, almonds, breadcrumbs, flour, baking powder, cinnamon, salt, and mace until well blended. Stir in suet. Stir in milk until all ingredients are moistened. Stir in egg yolks. Stir in reserved currant mixture. Gently fold in egg whites just until incorporated. Spoon mixture into prepared pudding mold and fasten the lid.

Put a steamer rack in a large kettle and set the mold on the rack. Add enough water to reach two-thirds of the way up the sides of the mold. Cover tightly and bring to a boil. Reduce heat to medium-low and steam for 2 1/2 hours, checking occasionally to make certain that the water is simmering and adding water if necessary. Remove from kettle and let cool.

To serve, unmold onto a serving plate. Drizzle top with remaining 3 tablespoons brandy immediately before serving and flambé if desired.

Serves 8 to 10
Serve with RMS Alambic Distillery
Special Reserve Brandy

WHITE CHOCOLATE & BRANDY TRUFFLES

A snifter of brandy and one of these
truffles is a grand way to end an evening.

6 ounces white chocolate, chopped

1/4 cup butter

3 tablespoons powdered sugar, sifted

1/4 cup heavy cream

1 tablespoon RMS Alambic Distillery Special
    Reserve Brandy

Unsweetened cocoa powder

In a bowl, combine chocolate, butter, and powdered sugar. In a small saucepan, bring cream to a boil over medium heat. Pour over chocolate mixture and whisk until smooth. Whisk in brandy. Cover and chill overnight.

Place cocoa powder in a shallow bowl. Remove chocolate mixture from the refrigerator. Using a melon baller, form mixture into balls about 1 inch in diameter. Roll in cocoa powder to coat. Place on a plate, cover, and store in the refrigerator. Let truffles stand at room temperature for about 10 minutes before serving.

Makes about 20 truffles
Serve with RMS Alambic Distillery
Special Reserve Brandy

CHOCOLATE
BREAD PUDDING

*I can't imagine a more sublime and exotic
way to use bread from the previous day.*

1 cup dried cherries

1/2 cup RMS Alambic Distillery Special
  Reserve Brandy

2 cups day-old French bread, crusts removed
  and cut into 1/2-inch cubes

1/2 cup slivered almonds

1 pound semisweet chocolate, chopped

6 eggs

1 cup sugar

2 cups heavy cream

1 teaspoon vanilla extract

1/8 teaspoon cinnamon

In a small bowl, combine dried cherries and
brandy, cover, and let sit overnight.

Preheat oven to 325° F. Lightly oil a 13 x 9-inch
baking dish.

Place bread cubes and almonds on a baking
sheet. Place in oven for about 5 to 10 minutes,
or until lightly toasted. Remove from oven and
set aside.

In the top of a double boiler, melt chocolate over simmering water. Whisk until smooth and let cool.

In a large bowl, beat eggs and sugar together until light and fluffy. Stir in cooled chocolate. Stir in cream, vanilla, and cinnamon until smooth. Stir in cherries and their liquid, toasted bread cubes, and almonds. Pour into prepared baking dish and let stand 30 minutes.

Bake for about 40 to 50 minutes, or until set in the middle and the pudding pulls away from the edges of the dish.

Serves 8 to 10
Serve with RMS Alambic Distillery
Special Reserve Brandy

KENTUCKY BLACK CAKE

The special flavors of this cake will pleasantly surprise and delight you and your guests. It's excellent as an afternoon treat with tea.

1¹/4 cups chopped dried figs

²/3 cup golden raisins

²/3 cup raisins

¹/2 cup RMS Alambic Distillery Special Reserve Brandy

¹/2 cup butter, softened

1¹/4 cups packed brown sugar

1¹/2 teaspoons cinnamon

³/4 teaspoon allspice

³/4 teaspoon cloves

³/4 teaspoon nutmeg

3 eggs

²/3 cup seedless blackberry jam

2¹/2 cups all-purpose flour

1¹/2 teaspoons baking soda

1¹/4 cups pecans, lightly toasted and chopped

🍂 In a shallow dish, combine figs, golden raisins, raisins, and brandy. Cover and let sit overnight.

Preheat oven to 325° F. Butter and flour two 8 1/2 x 4 1/2-inch loaf pans.

In a large bowl, cream butter until light. Add brown sugar, cinnamon, allspice, cloves, and nutmeg and beat until smooth. Add eggs, one at a time, beating well after each addition. Stir in jam until smooth. Sift the flour and baking soda together and add to the bowl. Beat until smooth, scraping sides often. Stir in the fig mixture and pecans until well blended. Divide batter between the prepared loaf pans. Bake for about 55 minutes, or until a toothpick inserted in the center comes out clean. Cool on racks.

Makes 2 loaves
Serve with RMS Alambic Distillery
Special Reserve Brandy

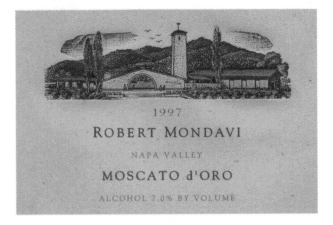

1997

ROBERT MONDAVI

NAPA VALLEY

MOSCATO d'ORO

ALCOHOL 7.0% BY VOLUME

ROBERT MONDAVI
WINERY

Founded in 1966 by Robert Mondavi and his son, Michael, the Robert Mondavi Winery is considered a leader in the modern wine industry. They are committed to producing naturally balanced wines of great finesse and elegance that complement and enhance fine food. They have been successful in achieving these goals through earth-friendly farming practices, a sophisticated winery emphasizing gentle treatment of their wines, and a genuine love for their handiwork. No other winery epitomizes the Napa Valley like the Robert Mondavi Winery.

LEMON
PANNA COTTA

*This fresh and vibrant dessert from
Sarah Scott would be excellent
after a meal of barbecued fish and
summer vegetables.*

2 cups buttermilk, divided

1 1/2 teaspoons unflavored gelatin

2/3 cup heavy cream

3/4 cup sugar, divided

3 tablespoons minced lemon zest

3/4 cup freshly squeezed lemon juice

1/2 teaspoon vanilla extract

Pour 1 cup of the buttermilk into the top of a
double boiler. Sprinkle gelatin over and let it soften
for about 5 minutes.

In a saucepan, stir together cream, 1/2 cup of the
sugar, and lemon zest. Bring to a boil, then pour into
the buttermilk mixture and whisk to blend.

In a small saucepan, stir together the lemon
juice and remaining 1/4 cup of the sugar. Bring to a
boil over medium-high heat, and cook until mixture is reduced to a thick syrup. Whisk lemon syrup
into the buttermilk mixture.

(recipe continued on next page)

Place the buttermilk mixture over simmering water, and cook, whisking constantly until gelatin dissolves. Whisk in remaining 1 cup buttermilk and vanilla. Pour into six (4-ounce) ramekins. Cover and chill at least 4 hours or overnight.

Serves 6
Serve with Robert Mondavi Winery
Moscato D'Oro

Wine comes in at the mouth
And love comes in at the eye;
That's all we shall know for truth
Before we grow old and die.

Yeats

ESTATE BOTTLED

1997

SONOMA-CUTRER

RUSSIAN RIVER RANCHES

SONOMA COAST CHARDONNAY BOTTLED BY SONOMA-CUTRER, WINDSOR, CA. TABLE WINE

SONOMA-CUTRER
VINEYARDS

Founded in January 1973 by Brice Cutrer Jones and Kent Klineman, Sonoma-Cutrer has focused solely on the production of outstanding Chardonnay from its vineyards in the Sonoma Coast Viticultural Appellation. To achieve their goal of producing the highest quality wine, they have selected hillside and rocky soils and planted them with the newest high-quality Dijon clones of Chardonnay. They are densely planted on low-vigor rootstocks and are trellised in traditional Burgundian fashion. Extended underground aging of the wines in proprietary French oak barrels produces wines of distinction and character.

RED PEAR
TART

With its topping of thinly sliced and fanned pears, this tart is as beautiful to look at as it is to eat.

CRUST:

1 cup all-purpose flour

2 tablespoons sugar

1/4 teaspoon salt

1/3 cup cold butter, cut into pieces

1 egg yolk

1 tablespoon cold water

1 teaspoon vanilla extract

FILLING:

2 tablespoons butter

2 tablespoons sugar

1 teaspoon all-purpose flour

1/2 teaspoon finely minced lemon zest

1/4 teaspoon cardamom

1/8 teaspoon salt

3 red pears, peeled, cored, and thinly sliced

🍇 Preheat oven to 375° F.

For the crust: In a bowl, stir together the flour, sugar, and salt. Cut in the butter until mixture resembles coarse meal. In a small bowl, whisk together egg yolk, water, and vanilla. Add to flour mixture and stir until dough holds together. Gather dough into a ball and flatten into a disk. Cover with plastic and chill.

For the filling: In a bowl, combine butter, sugar, flour, lemon zest, cardamom, and salt. Stir together with a fork until blended.

Turn dough out onto a lightly floured surface and roll out to fit into a 9-inch tart pan with a removable bottom. Sprinkle the filling evenly over the bottom of the crust. Fan pears and place on the crust. Bake for about 35 to 40 minutes, or until crust is golden brown.

Serves 6
Serve with Sonoma-Cutrer Vineyards
Chardonnay

STONE CREEK WINERY

Stone Creek's Tasting Room is located in Kenwood in the heart of Sonoma County, in what was once a one-room schoolhouse. This historical building was erected in 1890, and was one of the first public schools in the Los Guilicos Valley. In addition to its colorful history, the "Old Blue Schoolhouse" is now the happy home of Stone Creek Wines.

PUMPKIN AND GINGER CHEESECAKE
with Chocolate & Gingersnap Crust

Marc Downie of Catering by Design
came up with this autumnal cheesecake.

CRUST:

1 cup chocolate cookie crumbs

1 cup gingersnap cookie crumbs

1/4 cup butter, melted

FILLING:

2 pounds cream cheese, at room temperature

1 1/2 cups sugar

3 tablespoons all-purpose flour

1/4 cup finely grated ginger

2 teaspoons cinnamon

4 eggs

1 (15-ounce) can pumpkin

2 teaspoons vanilla extract

(recipe continued on next page)

🐝 Preheat oven to 350° F.

For the crust: In the bowl of a food processor, combine chocolate cookie crumbs and gingersnap crumbs and pulse a few times to mix. Add the melted butter and pulse to blend. Press the mixture into the bottom and 1 inch up the sides of a 10-inch spring-form pan. Place pan on a baking sheet and bake for about 8 minutes to set the crust. Remove from oven and set aside.

For the filling: In a large bowl, beat together the cream cheese and sugar until smooth. Beat in flour, ginger, and cinnamon. Add eggs, one at a time, beating well after each addition, scraping the bowl often. Stir in pumpkin and vanilla until well blended. Pour filling into crust. Place springform pan in a large baking pan and add enough water to come 1 inch up the side of the springform pan. Bake for about 1 hour and 15 minutes, or until cheesecake begins to pull away from the sides of the pan and is set in the middle. Cool to room temperature, then cover and chill overnight.

Remove cheesecake from the refrigerator. Run a knife around the side of the cheesecake and carefully remove the band of the springform pan. Carefully slide a long spatula under the crust of the cheesecake and slide onto a serving platter.

Serves 12
Serve with Stone Creek Winery
Gewürztraminer

ESTATE BOTTLED

Sullivan Vineyards

RUTHERFORD

1996 Napa Valley
Merlot

Estate Grown, Produced and Bottled
by Sullivan Vineyards Winery
Rutherford, California
Alcohol 13% by Volume
Contains Sulfites

SULLIVAN VINEYARDS

Jim Sullivan, owner and winemaker, produced his first vintage in 1962, while working as a graphic artist. Although now consumed entirely by his winery, he still takes the time to design his own labels and artwork. This meticulous attention to detail is evident throughout the winery, from the graceful vineyards and manicured lawns, which he personally attends, to the inky and magnificent wines he produces. "Creativity and perfection in all realms of living is what the Sullivans strive for," says Jim. "We don't stop when we put the brush down, but continue throughout our lives, in winemaking, in cooking, in friendships...it's what we're about."

POUND CAKE

A classic example of a finely textured pound cake, this rendition is superb with afternoon tea.

1 cup butter, softened

1 cup superfine sugar

4 eggs

2 teaspoons vanilla extract

2^{1}/4 cups sifted cake flour

1 teaspoon baking powder

^{1}/4 teaspoon salt

^{1}/4 cup milk

Preheat oven to 325° F. Butter and flour a 9^{1}/2 x 5^{1}/2-inch loaf pan.

In a bowl, beat the butter and sugar together for about 5 minutes, or until very pale and fluffy. Add eggs, one at a time, beating well after each addition. Beat in the vanilla. In a bowl, sift together the flour, baking powder, and salt. Add flour mixture to the butter mixture alternately with the milk, beginning and ending with the flour mixture. Spread batter into the prepared loaf pan. Bake for about 65 to 70 minutes, or until a toothpick inserted in the center comes out clean. Cool in the pan for 15 minutes, then turn out onto a rack to cool completely.

Serves 8

Serve with Sullivan Vineyards Merlot

STONEGATE WINERY

Steep slopes, shallow, stony loam soil, and excellent drainage force the vines in Stonegate's vineyards to compete intensely with each other. The results are clearly visible in the reds from these vineyards. Cabernet Sauvignon, Merlot, and Cabernet Franc exhibit excellent structure, dark color, and long, lingering finishes. At their best when paired with a fine meal, the wines are full of nuance and flavor. The Chardonnay, planted at the extreme north end of the Napa Valley in the hillside Bella Vista Vineyard, is multilayered and chockfull of ripe fruit aromas. Stonegate's Estate Bottled Sauvignon Blanc and Late Harvest Dessert Wine come from the vineyard surrounding the winery.

CHOCOLATE CABERNET CAKE

Nicholas Johnson from Piper Johnson Catering
graciously shared his secret for his sinfully rich cake.

CHOCOLATE CABERNET CAKE:

3 tablespoons minced dried apricots

1/4 cup Stonegate Winery Cabernet Sauvignon

1/4 teaspoon almond extract

1/2 cup butter

6 ounces semisweet chocolate

3 egg yolks

3/4 cup sugar, divided

2/3 cup ground blanched almonds

1/4 cup all-purpose flour

3 egg whites

1/4 teaspoon cream of tartar

GLAZE:

1/2 cup butter

6 ounces semisweet chocolate

1 tablespoon corn syrup

Preheat oven to 375° F. Butter an 8-inch cake pan, line the bottom with parchment paper, and butter the parchment.

(recipe continued on next page)

For the cake: In a small bowl, combine apricots, wine, and almond extract. Set aside. In the top of a double boiler, melt butter and chocolate together over simmering water. Whisk until smooth and let cool.

In a large bowl, beat egg yolks and $1/2$ cup of the sugar together until pale in color and thick. Fold in the chocolate mixture and ground almonds. Add the reserved apricot mixture. Sift the flour over the batter and fold together. In a bowl, beat the egg whites until foamy. Add the cream of tartar and beat until soft peaks form. Gradually beat in the remaining $1/4$ cup sugar, and continue to beat until stiff but not dry. Gently but thoroughly fold the egg white mixture into the batter. Pour batter into prepared pan and bake for about 40 minutes, or until a toothpick inserted in the center comes out clean. Cool in the pan. Run a knife around the edge of the cake, invert onto an 8-inch round of cardboard, and peel off the parchment. Wrap in plastic wrap and chill overnight.

For the glaze: In the top of a double boiler, melt butter and chocolate together over simmering water. Remove from heat and whisk in corn syrup until smooth.

Place cake on a rack set on a baking sheet. Brush off any crumbs. With a small spatula, spread the glaze over the top and sides of the cake. Pour remaining glaze over the top evenly. Chill to set the glaze.

Serves 10
Serve with Stonegate Winery
Cabernet Sauvignon

PLUM & RASPBERRY SORBET

Frozen sorbets are one of the quintessential pleasures of summer in the wine country. Serve this cooling dessert after a hot day in the vineyard...or in the garden.

1 cup sugar

$1/2$ cup water

$1/4$ cup Stonegate Winery Cabernet Sauvignon

$1 1/2$ pounds plums, pitted and sliced

$2 1/2$ cups raspberries

$1/4$ teaspoon freshly squeezed lemon juice

In a saucepan, combine sugar, water, and wine. Simmer over low heat until sugar dissolves. Bring to a boil and cook for 1 minute. Remove from heat and cool to room temperature.

Combine plums and raspberries in the bowl of a food processor. Process until smooth. Strain purée through a sieve into a large bowl. Press on the solids to extract as much juice as possible. Discard the solids.

Stir in sugar syrup and lemon juice until well blended. Chill thoroughly then pour mixture into an ice-cream maker and freeze according to manufacturer's directions.

Makes about 1 quart
Serve with Stonegate Winery
Cabernet Sauvignon

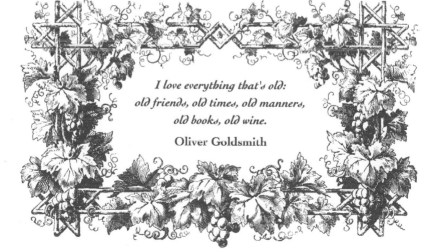

I love everything that's old:
old friends, old times, old manners,
old books, old wine.
Oliver Goldsmith

TOPOLOS RUSSIAN RIVER VINEYARDS

Topolos Russian River Vineyards is a family-owned winery and restaurant in Sonoma County just an hour north of San Francisco and fifteen minutes west of Santa Rosa. Whether you choose to dine outside around the fountain patio or inside by the fireplace, Russian River Vineyards is the ultimate Sonoma County winery experience. The ambience is casual but elegant, and the menus combine authentic Greek cuisine from the Topolos family's recipes with offerings from the rest of the Mediterranean and the chef's creative inventions.

CHOCOLATE MARQUISE

This trufflelike cake from Bob Engle is incredibly rich and decadent—and it really shines with a glass of Cabernet Sauvignon.

14 ounces bittersweet chocolate,
  finely chopped

2/3 cup butter, softened

5 egg yolks

3 tablespoons Frangelico liqueur

1/4 cup heavy cream, whipped

5 egg whites, beaten until stiff but not dry

Raspberries for garnish

Line the bottom and sides of a 9 1/2 x 5 1/2-inch loaf pan with parchment paper.

In the top of a double boiler, melt chocolate over barely simmering water. Remove from heat and whisk until smooth. Let cool slightly.

In a large bowl, beat butter until fluffy. Add egg yolks, one at a time, beating well after each addition. Beat in the liqueur. Stir in the chocolate until smooth. Gently fold in the whipped cream. Gently but thoroughly fold in the egg whites. Spread the batter into the prepared loaf pan. Cover and chill overnight.

(recipe continued on next page)

To serve, invert onto a serving plate and tap until cake releases. Peel off paper. Slice about 1 inch thick and place on chilled plates. Sprinkle with fresh raspberries.

Serves 8
Serve with Topolos Russian River Vineyards
Cabernet Sauvignon

A feast of fat things,
a feast of wine on the lees.
The Bible

DUCKHORN VINEYARDS

When your last name is Duckhorn, it stands to reason that you would choose a duck to be a symbol for your winery. Dan and Margaret Duckhorn have taken that theme and created one of the Napa Valley's most respected premium wineries. Hand-harvested and sorted grapes enter their crusher to emerge as ultra-premium Cabernets, Merlots, Zinfandels and Sauvignon blancs. New vineyards in Mendocino's Anderson Valley promise to deliver world-class Pinot noirs to their flock of stylistic wines.

MIEL-GLAZED
APRICOT TART
with Macadamia Crust

'Miel' is the French word for 'honey', and it is also the name of a heavenly dessert wine from Duckhorn Vineyards.

MACADAMIA CRUST:

1 cup macadamias

1 1/2 cups all-purpose flour

1/2 cup cold butter, cut into small pieces

1/4 cup sugar

1/8 teaspoon salt

1 egg

1 teaspoon vanilla extract

FILLING:

1 pound apricots, peeled, pitted, and sliced

1/2 cup sugar

1/4 cup heavy cream

1/4 cup milk

1 egg

1/4 teaspoon almond extract

GLAZE:

1/2 cup powdered sugar

1 tablespoon Duckhorn Vineyards Miel

For the crust: Place macadamias in the bowl of a food processor and process until finely ground. Add flour, butter, sugar, and salt and process until mixture resembles coarse meal. Add egg and vanilla and pulse until mixture comes together and is evenly moistened. Press mixture firmly into the bottom and up the sides of a 9-inch tart pan with a removable bottom. Chill for 1 hour.

Preheat oven to 400° F.

Bake tart crust in the middle of the oven for 20 to 25 minutes, or until golden brown. Remove from oven and cool slightly.

For the filling: Arrange apricots in a spiral in the prebaked crust. In a small bowl, whisk together sugar, milk, heavy cream, egg, and almond extract until smooth. Pour mixture over apricots. Return to oven and bake an additional 25 to 30 minutes, or until custard is set. Remove from oven and cool.

For the glaze: In a small bowl, stir together powdered sugar and wine until smooth. Drizzle glaze over tart and serve in thin wedges.

Serves 8
Serve with Duckhorn Vineyards
Miel

TREFETHEN
VINEYARDS

Tradition combines with technology at Trefethen Vineyards, where a century-old winery and the latest in winemaking equipment give the Trefethen family, and their wines, the best of both worlds. First planted with grapes in the 1850s, the Eshcol ranch, as it was known back then, received its name from a biblical allusion to an immense cluster of grapes. In 1968, Gene and Katie Trefethen revitalized the old Eshcol property and planted new vines on the 600-acre valley estate and on fifty acres to the northwest. The first wines were vinified in 1973, and today wine production has climbed to 75,000 cases per year. The Trefethen family has this to say about their wines: "Winemaking is part agriculture and part parenting. We are proud to introduce you to what we have worried over and cared for—our wines. They are meant to be shared and enjoyed among friends."

FROZEN MEYER LEMON SOUFFLÉ

If you can't find the truly incredible Meyer lemon in your area, use regular lemons instead.

^{1}/3 cup freshly squeezed Meyer lemon juice

1 cup sugar, divided

4 egg yolks

1 teaspoon vanilla extract

2 cups heavy cream

In a small saucepan, stir together lemon juice and ^{1}/4 cup of the sugar. Simmer over medium heat until mixture is thick and syrupy. Remove from heat and let cool.

In a bowl, combine egg yolks and 2 tablespoons of the sugar and beat until thick and pale colored. Beat in vanilla and cooled lemon syrup.

In a large bowl, beat cream until soft peaks form. Add sugar slowly and continue to beat until sugar has dissolved. Gently but thoroughly fold lemon mixture into whipped cream. Pour mixture into a 1^1/2 quart soufflé dish, cover, and freeze overnight.

Serves 6 to 8
Serve with Trefethen Vineyards
Chardonnay

TURNBULL
WINE CELLARS

Just south of Oakville in the Napa Valley, Patrick O'Dell, proprietor of Turnbull Wine Cellars, produces stunning wines of amazing complexity and depth. His well-known red wines include Cabernet Sauvignon, Merlot, and Sangiovese, as well as small amounts of Syrah and Zinfandel. A limited amount of elegant Sauvignon Blanc is a special treat for white-wine lovers who visit his tasting room.

BAKED PERSIMMON PUDDING

Orange persimmons hanging heavy from leafless trees are a sign of the end of the harvest season and the beginning of winter. Beverley Wolfe gave us this recipe to help us enjoy nature's golden fall bounty.

2 pounds very ripe Hachiya persimmons

3 eggs

$^1/_2$ cup sugar

$^1/_4$ cup packed brown sugar

$1^1/_2$ cups milk

$^1/_4$ cup heavy cream

$1^1/_4$ cups all-purpose flour

$^3/_4$ teaspoon baking powder

$^3/_4$ teaspoon baking soda

$^3/_4$ teaspoon cardamom

1 cup chopped pecans, lightly toasted

$^1/_3$ cup butter, melted

Whipped cream

(recipe continued on next page)

Preheat oven to 350° F. Butter a 9-inch spring-form pan and line the bottom with parchment paper.

Peel the persimmons and purée flesh in a food processor. Pour purée into a large bowl. Add eggs, sugar, and brown sugar and beat until smooth. Stir in milk and cream. In a separate bowl, sift together flour, baking powder, baking soda, and cardamom. Add flour mixture to persimmon mixture and stir until well blended. Stir in pecans and melted butter. Pour batter into prepared pan. Bake for about 2 hours, or until pudding has set in the middle. Remove from oven and cool in the pan. Serve warm with whipped cream.

Serves 10
Serve with Turnbull Wine Cellars
Sauvignon Blanc

VIANSA WINERY

On the evening of January 29, 1988, on a hill near Sonoma, Sam and Vicki Sebastiani opened a bottle of sparkling wine and toasted the land that would one day see their dream a reality. Their winery, Viansa, would embody a proud Italian heritage, and it would overlook a lowland shared by vineyards and nearly 100 acres of restored natural wetlands. Today, Viansa is a reality welcoming visitors from around the world, and they invite you to share your wedding, special event, or meeting with them. The wines and food of Viansa are among the world's finest, and the wetlands provide critical habitat to countless waterfowl, animals, and aquatic life.

PARTY BISCOTTI
with Dried Fruits

Vicki Sebastiani, author of **Cucina Viansa,**
gave us this recipe for her special biscotti.

1/4 cup butter, softened

1 cup sugar

1 teaspoon baking powder

1/2 teaspoon baking soda

1/4 teaspoon salt

3 eggs

1/2 teaspoon vanilla extract

1/4 teaspoon almond extract

2 1/4 cups all-purpose flour

1 1/2 teaspoons anise seed

1/2 teaspoon fennel seed

1 cup dried cranberries

3/4 cup shelled pistachios

1/2 cup finely diced dried apricots

1 egg

1 tablespoon water

In a large bowl, beat butter for about 30 seconds. Add sugar, baking powder, baking soda, and salt and beat until smooth. Add 3 of the eggs, vanilla, and almond extract and beat until smooth. Add the flour and beat until you have a stiff dough. Stir in anise, fennel, cranberries, pistachios, and apricots. Form into a ball, cover, and chill until firm. In a small bowl, whisk together the remaining egg and water to make an egg wash.

Preheat oven to 350° F. Lightly oil a baking sheet. Divide the dough into two portions. Shape into logs 12 inches long. Place on prepared baking sheet and flatten slightly. Brush the tops of the dough with the egg wash. Bake for about 25 to 30 minutes, or until golden brown. Remove from oven and let cool for 1 hour.

Reduce oven temperature to 325° F. Transfer biscotti logs to a cutting board and cut into 1/2-inch thick diagonal slices. Place the biscotti, cut-side-down, on the baking sheet and bake 5 minutes. Turn biscotti over and bake an additional 5 minutes. Cool on racks.

Makes about 48 biscotti
Serve with Viansa Winery
Regalo di Grappa

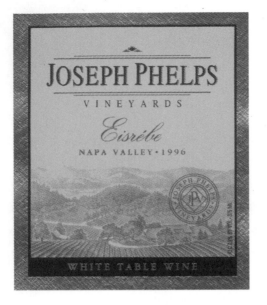

JOSEPH PHELPS
VINEYARDS

*Few wineries in Northern California have more
"firsts" to their name than the winery of Joseph Phelps.
"Insignia", the first Bordeaux-style blend to be produced in California as a proprietary wine ushered in
the era of the "Meritage" wines. His 1974 Syrah was
perhaps the first time that variety had been bottled as
such. And since 1990, his Vin du Mistral wines have
epitomized the classic Rhone varietals.*

*Located in a stunning, redwood building, the win-
ery is anchored to the landscape by a massive wiste-
ria-covered trellis made from 100-year-old recycled
bridge timbers. It is definitely worth an appointment
to visit this pioneer in the Napa Valley.*

ROASTED BANANA CHEESECAKE

*Roasting intensifies the flavor
of the bananas and adds a wonderful
depth of flavor to the cheesecake.*

3 ripe bananas, unpeeled

CRUST:

2 cups (8 ounces) vanilla wafer cookie crumbs

1/2 cup packed brown sugar

1/3 cup melted butter

FILLING:

1 1/2 pounds cream cheese

3/4 cup sugar

5 eggs

1 tablespoon dark rum

1 teaspoon vanilla extract

Preheat oven to 400° F.

Place the unpeeled bananas on a baking sheet and bake until they turn black all over, about 12 to 15 minutes. Cool, then remove and discard peels. Set aside.

(recipe continued on next page)

For the crust: Combine the cookie crumbs and brown sugar in the bowl of a food processor. Pulse a few times to mix ingredients. Add the butter and pulse to blend. Press mixture into the bottom of a 10-inch springform pan.

For the filling: In a large bowl, beat the cream cheese and sugar together until smooth, scraping the sides often. Add the eggs, one at a time, beating well after each addition. Add the roasted bananas, rum, and vanilla and beat until smooth.

Reduce oven temperature to 350° F.

Pour the batter into the prepared crust and place springform pan on a baking sheet. Bake for about 1 hour, or until cheesecake is very lightly golden and begins to pull away from the sides of the pan. Cool to room temperature, then cover and chill overnight.

Serves 12
Serve with Joseph Phelps Vineyards
Eisrebe

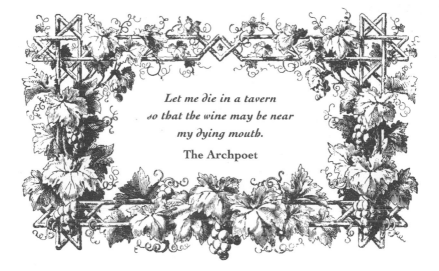

Let me die in a tavern
so that the wine may be near
my dying mouth.

The Archpoet

THE WINERIES:

Alderbrook Winery
2306 Magnolia Drive
Healdsburg, CA 95448
707.433.9154

Arrowood Vineyards and Winery
14347 Sonoma Highway
Glen Ellen, CA 95442
707.938.5170

Belvedere Vineyards and Winery
435 West Dry Creek Road
Healdsburg, CA 95448
707.433.8236

Brutocao Cellars
7000 Highway 128
Philo, CA 95466
707.744.1664

Cakebread Cellars
8300 St. Helena Highway
Rutherford, CA 94573
707.963.5221

Cedar Mountain Winery
7000 Tesla Road
Livermore, CA 94550
510.373.6694

Clos Pegase Winery
1060 Dunaweal Lane
Calistoga, CA 94515
707.942.4981

De Loach Vineyards
1791 Olivet Road
Santa Rosa, CA 95401
707.526.91111

Domaine Charbay Winery
and Distillery
4001 Spring Mountain Road
St. Helena, CA 94574
707.963.9327

Duckhorn Vineyards
1000 Lodi Lane
St. Helena, CA 94574
707.963.7108

Dry Creek Vineyard
3770 Lambert Bridge Road
Healdsburg, CA 95448
707.433.1000

Ferrari-Carano Winery
8761 Dry Creek Road
Healdsburg, CA 95448
707.433.6700

Fetzer Vineyards
13601 Eastside Road
Hopland, CA 95449
707.744.7600

Gloria Ferrer Champagne Caves
23555 Highway 121
Sonoma, CA 95476
707.996.7256

Husch Vineyards
4400 Highway 128
Philo, CA 95466
707.462.5370

Iron Horse Vineyards
9786 Ross Station Road
Sebastopol, CA 95472
707.887.1507

Joseph Phelps Vineyards
200 Taplin Road
St. Helena, CA 94574
707.963.2745

Kendall-Jackson Wine Center
5007 Fulton Road
Santa Rosa, CA 95439
707.571.8100

Kenwood Vineyards
9592 Sonoma Highway
Kenwood, CA 95452
707.571.5891

Kunde Estate Winery
10155 Sonoma Highway
Kenwood, CA 95452
707.833.5501

Mark West Winery
7010 Trenton-Healdsburg Road
Forestville, CA 95436
707.544.4813

Markham Vineyards
2812 St. Helena Highway
St. Helena, CA 94574
707.963.5292

Martini & Prati Winery
2191 Laguna Road
Santa Rosa, CA 95401
707.823.2404

Monticello Vineyards
4242 Big Ranch Road
Napa, CA 94558
800.743.6668

Navarro Vineyards
5601 Highway 128
Philo, CA 95466
707.895.3686

RMS Alambic Distillery
1250 Cuttings Wharf Road
Napa, CA 94559
707.253.9055

Robert Mondavi Winery
7801 St. Helena Highway
Oakville, CA 94562
707.226.1395

Sonoma Cutrer Vineyards
4401 Slusser Road
Windsor, CA 95492
707.528.1561

Stone Creek Winery
9380 Sonoma Highway
Kenwood, CA 95452
707.833.4455

Stonegate Winery
183 Dunaweal Lane
Calistoga, CA 94515
707.942.6500

Sullivan Vineyards
1090 Galleron Road
Rutherford, CA 94573
707.963.9646

Topolos at Russian River
5700 Gravenstein Highway, North
Forestville, CA 95436
707.887.1575

Trefethen Vineyards
1160 Oak Knoll Avenue
Napa, CA 94558
707.255.7700

Turnbull Wine Cellars
8210 St. Helena Highway
Oakville, CA 94562
800.887.6285

Viansa Winery
25200 Arnold Drive
Sonoma, CA 95476
707.935.4700

THE CATERERS:

Catering by Design
Post Office Box 1866
Glen Ellen, CA 95442
707.935.0390

Linda Thomas Catering
Napa Valley, CA
707.944.8096

Piper Johnson Catering
Napa Valley, CA
707.942.5432

Vinga Restaurant
320 Third Street
San Francisco, CA 94107
415.546.3131

Conversions

LIQUID

1 tablespoon = 15 milliliters

1/2 cup = 4 fluid ounces = 125 milliliters

1 cup = 8 fluid ounces = 250 milliliters

DRY

1/4 cup = 4 tablespoons = 2 ounces = 60 grams

1 cup = 1/2 pound = 8 ounces = 250 grams

FLOUR

1/2 cup = 60 grams

1 cup = 4 ounces = 125 grams

TEMPERATURE

400 degrees F = 200 degrees C = gas mark 6

375 degrees F = 190 degrees C = gas mark 5

350 degrees F = 175 degrees C = gas mark 4

MISCELLANEOUS

2 tablespoons butter = 1 ounce = 30 grams